D0769491

WITHDRAWN

A GIFT FROM THE
FRIENDS OF THE
PLEASANT HILL LIBRARY

ANACONDAS

by Josh Gregory

Children's Press®

An Imprint of Scholastic Inc.

Content Consultant
Dr. Stephen S. Ditchkoff
Professor of Wildlife Sciences
Auburn University
Auburn, Alabama

Photographs ©: cover: chamleunejai/Shutterstock, Inc.; 1: Rliniger/
Dreamstime; 2 background, 3 background: Patricia Hofmeester/
Dreamstime; 2, 3 inset: Daniel Heuclin/Minden Pictures; 4, 5
background: Nick Garbutt/Minden Pictures; 5 inset top: Ishara
S. Kodikara/AFP/Getty Images; 5 inset bottom: Minden Pictures/
Superstock, Inc.; 6, 7: Colette6/Dreamstime; 8, 9: Ingo Arndt/
Minden Pictures/National Geographic Creative; 10, 11: Daniel
Heuclin/Minden Pictures; 12, 13: Franco Banfi/Getty Images; 14,
15: Yoshiharu Sekino/Science Source; 16, 17: Gunter Ziesler/Getty
Images; 18, 19: chamleunejai/Shutterstock, Inc.; 20, 21: Francois
Gohier/Science Source; 22, 23: blickwinkel/Alamy Images; 24,
25: Francois Savigny/Minden Pictures; 26, 27: Ishara S. Kodikara/
AFP/Getty Images; 28, 29: Dr. Morley Read/Shutterstock, Inc.; 30,
31: WaterFrame/Alamy Images; 32, 33: Mark Kostich/iStockphoto;
34, 35: Nick Garbutt/Minden Pictures; 36, 37: Minden Pictures/
Superstock, Inc.; 38, 39: Bill Haber/AP Images; 40, 41: Pete
Oxford/Minden Pictures; 44, 45 background: Patricia Hofmeester/
Dreamstime; 46: Rliniger/Dreamstime.

Library of Congress Cataloging-in-Publication Data
Gregory, Josh, author.
  Anacondas / by Josh Gregory.
    pages cm. — (Nature's children)
  Summary: "This book details the life and habits of anacondas"—
Provided by publisher.
  Includes bibliographical references and index.
  ISBN 978-0-531-22719-0 (library binding) — ISBN 978-0-531-
22517-2 (pbk.)
  1. Anaconda—Juvenile literature. I. Title. II. Series: Nature's children
(New York, N.Y.)
  QL666.O63G74 2016
  597.96'7—dc23   2015020022

No part of this publication may be reproduced in whole or in part,
or stored in a retrieval system, or transmitted in any form or by any
means, electronic, mechanical, photocopying, recording, or otherwise,
without written permission of the publisher. For information regarding
permission, write to Scholastic Inc., Attention: Permissions Department,
557 Broadway, New York, NY 10012.
© 2016 Scholastic Inc.

All rights reserved. Published in 2016 by Children's Press, an imprint
of Scholastic Inc.

Printed in China 62
SCHOLASTIC, CHILDREN'S PRESS, and associated logos are
trademarks and/or registered trademarks of Scholastic Inc.

1 2 3 4 5 6 7 8 9 10 R 25 24 23 22 21 20 19 18 17 16

Anacondas

Class	Reptilia
Order	Squamata
Family	Boidae
Genus	*Eunectes*
Species	Four species
World distribution	Northern South America, east of the Andes Mountains
Habitat	Swamps, wetlands, in and around slow-moving bodies of water
Distinctive physical characteristics	Green anaconda is the largest snake species in the world; some may reach lengths of 20 feet (6 meters) or more and weigh more than 550 pounds (250 kilograms); other species are slightly smaller; females are generally larger than males; skin color is yellow, green, or brown with darker spots; exact coloration depends on species
Habits	Generally solitary; spends most of its time in the water; waits for prey to draw near, then strikes out to bite the animal; uses powerful body to coil around prey and crush it to death; swallows prey whole; mates in spring; females attract males using scents and airborne chemicals called pheromones; gives birth to anywhere from 24 to 80 live babies after a period of 6 to 10 months
Diet	Carnivorous; will attack anything from small reptiles or birds to deer, jaguars, and other large mammals

ANACONDAS

Contents

CHAPTER 1

Lying in Wait

It is evening in the Amazon rain forest. Though the sun is setting, there is plenty of activity in the dense plant growth. One of the many animals out this evening is a bulky, piglike **mammal** called a peccary. The peccary is trudging through the forest with its nose to the ground in search of plants to eat. Soon, it reaches a nearby stream. Deciding to take a drink, it approaches the water's edge.

Unfortunately for the peccary, a dangerous **predator** lies in wait beneath the surface of the murky water. As the peccary bends down to drink, a gargantuan snake suddenly bursts forward with its jaws wide open. It's an anaconda! The peccary fights back, but its efforts will not save it from this incredible predator. The snake bites down on the neck of its **prey**. Then it quickly wrestles the peccary down into the water by wrapping itself around the unlucky animal's body.

A yellow anaconda peeks above the water's surface as it swims.

Sizable Snakes

Anacondas are snakes that belong to the **genus** *Eunectes*. There are four different anaconda **species**. Though there are some differences between them, these snakes all share the same basic characteristics. They are large, powerful hunters that use their muscular bodies to **constrict** prey.

The most common anaconda species is the green anaconda. Also called the giant anaconda, it is the largest snake species in the world. An average green anaconda is around 16 feet (4.9 meters) long. However, some of these snakes grow to be much longer. The largest can weigh as much as 550 pounds (250 kilograms). They have been measured at more than 12 inches (30.5 centimeters) thick at the body's widest point. The anaconda's skin can be colored in many different shades of green. Oval-shaped black spots run along the length of its back, with smaller black-and-yellow spots along its sides.

Adult male
6 ft. (1.8 m)

Giant anaconda
16 ft. (4.9 m) long
12 in. (30.5 cm) wide

This green anaconda's coloring helps the snake blend into its rain forest surroundings.

Anaconda Varieties

The other three anaconda species are all smaller than the green anaconda. However, they are still very large compared to most other snakes. The Bolivian anaconda is similar to the green anaconda, but is slightly smaller and darker.

Yellow anacondas are named for their lighter skin color. They have yellow or gold skin and are covered in dark spots. Smaller than green or Bolivian anacondas, they reach a maximum length of about 10 feet (3 m). Though they aren't as well known as green anacondas, they are still fairly common.

The final anaconda species is the dark-spotted anaconda. As this snake's name implies, it has a darker skin color than other anacondas. It is usually dark brown with black spots. This snake is the least common type of anaconda. As a result, its habits have not been studied as widely as those of other anacondas.

FUN FACT! Each anaconda has a unique pattern of spots on the underside of its tail.

A dark-spotted anaconda rests in a tree in French Guiana.

Watery Homes

Anacondas are **aquatic** snakes. This means they live only in places where they can spend most of their time in the water. Such **habitats** include swamps and wetlands. Anacondas are also common in tropical rain forests, near streams where the water does not move too quickly.

All four anaconda species are **native** only to South America. Specifically, they can be found in the northern part of the continent, east of the Andes Mountains. Each species makes its home in a certain part of this range. The Bolivian anaconda can be found only in the country of Bolivia. The dark-spotted anaconda lives only in parts of Brazil, as well as Guyana and French Guiana. The yellow anaconda is more widespread. It is found throughout the country of Paraguay, as well as neighboring portions of Argentina, Bolivia, and Brazil. Green anacondas have the widest range of all. They occupy huge areas of South America, including the island of Trinidad.

Anacondas can swim far beneath the water's surface.

CHAPTER 2

Tougher Than the Rest

Anacondas are some of the strongest predators in their habitats. They are capable of taking down almost any kind of prey that comes near. They are not picky when it comes to choosing their meals either. Even some of the largest species in South America are on the menu for anacondas. This includes animals that weigh up to 50 percent of an anaconda's own body weight. Mammals such as deer, wild pigs, and capybaras all serve as prey for anacondas. Caimans, which are similar to alligators, are another food that anacondas eat regularly. Smaller animals such as birds, fish, turtles, and lizards are common prey for younger anacondas. When live prey is scarce, anacondas sometimes also eat **carrion**.

Eating such a diet helps anacondas grow to their tremendous sizes. In turn, the larger an anaconda is, the larger the prey it is able to catch and eat.

An anaconda in the Orinoco River in Venezuela captures a caiman for a meal.

Specialized Skills

Anacondas are built to thrive in their aquatic homes. They spend almost all of their time in water. There, they are able to stay hidden and move quickly by swimming. Their coloring and patterned skin make them difficult to see from above. An anaconda's eyes and nostrils are on the top of its head. This allows the snake to keep a close eye on its surroundings while remaining almost entirely submerged.

Because anacondas are so long and heavy, they are much slower and clumsier on land than in water. However, they often slither up onto dry ground to rest in the warmth of the sunlight. On land, an anaconda might stretch out along a riverbank or climb up into the branches of a nearby tree. Such positions allow the snake to quickly drop back into the water if it needs to.

FUN FACT! Small anacondas sometimes climb trees to eat eggs from birds' nests.

Despite its large size, an anaconda can remain well-hidden in water.

Deadly Maneuvers

Anacondas do not actively search out their prey. Instead, they remain hidden underwater, waiting for prey to come to them. An animal may swim nearby or approach the edge of the water to drink or take a bath. Then the anaconda is ready to strike. In the blink of an eye, it springs forward and bites down on its prey. An anaconda's teeth are shaped like curved needles. They also point backward. This makes it very difficult for prey to pull away once the anaconda bites.

Unlike some other snakes, anacondas do not have a poisonous bite. Instead, they must rely on their strength to finish killing an animal. This is particularly true for very large prey. Once an anaconda has bitten down, it begins wrapping its long, powerful body around its victim. As it does so, it squeezes its strong muscles and pulls the prey underwater. Sometimes the prey dies because the constriction keeps it from breathing. Other times, it simply drowns.

An anaconda opens its mouth wide as it prepares to strike.

Time to Eat

An anaconda knows that its prey has died when the animal stops struggling. At this point, the snake begins to unwrap itself from the animal's body. If it has not yet managed to pull the prey into the water, the snake usually does so once the kill is completed. It then positions the prey's body so it can be swallowed headfirst. No matter how large an anaconda's meal is, it does not chew it. To fit the prey into its mouth, the anaconda's jaws can stretch extremely wide. As the snake swallows, its entire body expands. An anaconda that has recently eaten a large meal might display a very large bulge in its midsection.

An anaconda's feeding process is much simpler when the snake is dealing with smaller prey. In these cases, the anaconda does not need to rely on constriction. It can simply kill the prey with its powerful bite and swallow it right away.

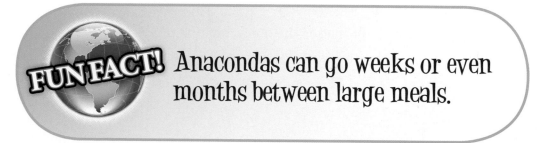

FUN FACT! Anacondas can go weeks or even months between large meals.

It is easy to spot the bulge in the body of an anaconda that has recently swallowed a large meal.

Formidable Foes

As top predators in their environment, anacondas face few natural threats in the wild. The biggest risks come while an anaconda is still growing. A number of animals prey on younger anacondas. These include many species that become prey for fully grown anacondas. Foxes, caimans, and a variety of predatory birds all hunt small anacondas. Sometimes the young snakes are even eaten by other anacondas. To defend itself, an anaconda might roll up into a ball to guard its head. It can then strike out when it sees an opportunity.

Even adult anacondas sometimes end up in dangerous situations. They prey upon any animal that draws near. As a result, the snakes sometimes become locked in battle with equally fierce opponents. For example, anacondas might attack or be attacked by jaguars. These strong cats do not go down without a fight. Caimans are also capable of defending themselves from anaconda attacks. No matter the outcome, one powerful predator will end up becoming prey for another.

A burrowing owl swoops down to attack an anaconda in Brazil.

CHAPTER 3

An Anaconda's Life

Anacondas are **solitary** animals. Because they would compete with one another for food, they rarely spend much time together. However, one exception to this lifestyle comes every spring, for a period of several weeks in April and May. This is the anaconda's **breeding** season.

During this time, female anacondas begin leaving scent trails on the ground as they move around. They also release special chemicals called pheromones into the air. Males detect these chemicals by flicking their tongues in and out of their mouths. They follow these signals to find the nearby female.

Several males might try to **mate** with the same female. In these situations, they all wrap themselves together in a ball around the female. There might be as many as 12 males in one of these "breeding balls." They stay wrapped together for up to four weeks. Some experts believe the males are slowly wrestling each other to determine which one will mate with the female.

Several male anacondas wrap themselves around
a single large female when forming a mating ball.

Born Alive

After mating, male and female anacondas generally go their separate ways. However, the female might eat her mate before he has a chance to get away. She will not eat during her pregnancy, so this meal provides her with important nutrients.

An anaconda's pregnancy lasts between 6 and 10 months. Unlike many other types of snakes, anacondas do not lay eggs. Instead, each baby develops in a clear, egg-like sac inside the mother's body. This keeps the developing babies warm and safe from threats.

When it is time for the babies to be born, their mother pushes them out of her body through an opening called the **cloaca**. She gives birth to anywhere from 24 to 80 babies at once. The babies are still inside their sacs when they are born, and they must quickly break free.

FUN FACT! Female anacondas are usually larger than males.

Baby anacondas look like small versions of adult anacondas.

Starting Out Small

Once anaconda babies are born, their mother leaves them. The young snakes must fend for themselves. However, the babies are not defenseless. They know how to swim and hunt for food almost immediately.

Anacondas are between 12 and 24 inches (30.5 and 61 cm) long at birth. Because of this small size, many young anacondas become prey for other hunters. As the snakes grow larger, however, they become better at fending off attackers. Like other snakes, anacondas shed their skins regularly as they grow. They also grow very quickly. By the time an anaconda is three years old, it is likely to be about 10 feet (3 m) long.

Male anacondas begin mating and producing young once they are about 18 months old. Females take roughly twice as long to start having babies of their own. On average, an anaconda is likely to live for about 10 years in the wild. However, some have been known to survive more than twice as long.

An anaconda's skin becomes dull and grayish just before it is shed.

CHAPTER 4

The Family Tree

Snakes' long, limbless bodies, unblinking eyes, and fast-moving forked tongues give them an appearance that is distinct from that of other **reptiles**. However, snakes did not always look like this. Their early **ancestors** probably looked something like today's lizards, with legs and shorter bodies.

The first true snakes probably appeared sometime between 174 million and 163 million years ago. Scientists have learned about these ancient species by studying **fossils**. The oldest known snake fossil was discovered in England. It dates back around 167 million years. Fossils reveal how some species have changed over time. They also show evidence of species that have disappeared.

There are almost 3,000 snake species living today. They vary widely in size and appearance, and they live in many different types of environments. While all snakes are predators, one species' diet might be entirely different from that of another.

Fossils of ancient boas have been found in many places, including Wyoming.

All about Boas

Anacondas belong to a family of snakes known as boas. There are about 40 different boa species, and they all share the same basic characteristics with anacondas. For example, boas are never poisonous, and they all rely on constriction to help them kill prey.

Some boas live in aquatic environments, as anacondas do. Others live in forests or even deserts. Instead of hiding in water, they crawl between rocks or peek out from beneath piles of leaves. Like anacondas, other boas are not very fast when moving on land. All boa species rely on surprise attacks to get the jump on their prey. Some species, such as the boa constrictor, hunt from trees. They climb up and hang from branches. When an animal passes by, they can reach out and bite it. Boa constrictors can even snatch bats and birds right out of the air as they fly by!

Boa constrictors spend a lot of their time in trees.

Large and Small

While green anacondas are the biggest snakes in the world, there are other snake species that are almost as large. The reticulated python is about the same length as the green anaconda. However, it is not as thick or as heavy. This doesn't stop it from being a deadly hunter. Like the green anaconda, this python is able to attack and constrict a wide variety of large prey.

Not all snakes are so large. The Barbados threadsnake is the smallest known snake species. It is just a few inches long and as thin as a spaghetti noodle. These tiny snakes are found only on the island of Barbados, where they burrow underground like earthworms. This lifestyle makes it difficult for scientists to study them. However, most experts believe that Barbados threadsnakes feed mainly on the **larvae** of burrowing insects such as ants or termites.

FUN FACT! Barbados threadsnakes were not recognized as a species until 2008.

A reticulated python's name comes from its reticulated, or netlike, color pattern.

CHAPTER 5

Humans and Anacondas

Like other large snakes, anacondas have a reputation for being dangerous to humans. In movies, TV shows, and other entertainment, anacondas are often portrayed as terrifying, man-eating monsters. As a result, many people are afraid of the snakes. These reptiles, however, don't really deserve this reputation. Though some scientists have reported incidents of anacondas killing humans, these snakes rarely attack people at all. Anacondas are generally so calm that some researchers can collect them for study by simply walking into their habitats and picking them up.

In fact, humans are much more dangerous to anacondas than the snakes are to people. Sometimes people hunt anacondas for their meat. The snakes' skins can also be valuable. They are used to make expensive shoes, bags, and clothing. Such hunting is often illegal, but that does not stop people who see the snakes as a way to make money.

Even when an anaconda is calm, it can take more than one person to capture the huge snake.

Alien Invaders

While snakes terrify some people, they fascinate others. As a result, people in many places want to keep anacondas and other exotic snakes as pets. The snakes are captured from their natural homes and shipped to people who live far away. Many people who purchase anacondas quickly find that they cannot provide the proper care for the animals. Because anacondas are so large, they require a lot of space. They also need a steady supply of meat to stay healthy.

Many pet owners soon tire of the difficulty and expense of these requirements. Some of these people release the snakes in wild areas nearby. For example, both green and yellow anacondas have been found living in parts of Florida. This has the potential to cause major problems for the area's native species. **Invasive** species can cause populations of certain prey species to decline. This puts those prey species in danger and lowers the food supply for local predators.

A man handles his pet anaconda in New Orleans, Louisiana.

Harm to Habitats

Throughout history, anacondas have not had to share much of their home with humans. They had plenty of space to hunt for food and reproduce. This is quickly changing in some habitats, however. As human populations increase, people need more space for farms. They also cut down more trees for use in wood and paper products. This is causing areas such as the Amazon rain forest to disappear little by little. The snakes will have less space to live, and there will be fewer prey animals for them to hunt.

Anacondas are not currently considered **endangered**. Yet there is no doubt that the habitats they and countless other species make home are disappearing. Additionally, as people move into more wild areas, they often kill anacondas and other snakes out of fear. In response, many organizations are working to spread the word about these amazing animals and the important role they play in the environment. Changes in the way people treat anacondas and their habitats are necessary to create a safe future for these snakes and other animals.

An anaconda's wild environment is complex and important.

Words to Know

ancestors (AN-ses-turz) — ancient animal species that are related to modern species

aquatic (uh-KWAH-tik) — living or growing in water

breeding (BREED-ing) — mating and giving birth to young

carrion (KAYR-ee-uhn) — flesh of dead animals

cloaca (kloh-AY-kuh) — the combined opening through which waste and reproductive substances exit the body in some animals

constrict (kuhn-STRIKT) — to squeeze

endangered (en-DAYN-jurd) — at risk of becoming extinct, usually because of human activity

fossils (FOSS-uhlz) — the hardened remains of prehistoric plants and animals

genus (JEE-nuhs) — a group of related plants or animals that is larger than a species but smaller than a family

habitats (HAB-uh-tats) — places where an animal or a plant is usually found

invasive (in-VAY-siv) — describing a plant or animal that is introduced to a new habitat and may cause that habitat harm

larvae (LAR-vee) — insects at the stage of development between an egg and a pupa, when it looks like a worm

mammal (MAM-uhl) — a warm-blooded animal that has hair or fur and usually gives birth to live young

mate (MAYT) — to join together to produce babies

native (NAY-tiv) — naturally belonging to a certain place

predator (PRED-uh-tur) — an animal that lives by hunting other animals for food

prey (PRAY) — an animal that's hunted by another animal for food

reptiles (REP-tilez) — cold-blooded animals that crawl across the ground or creep on short legs; they also have backbones and reproduce by laying eggs

solitary (SAH-li-ter-ee) — preferring to live alone

species (SPEE-sheez) — one of the groups into which animals and plants of the same genus are divided

Habitat Map

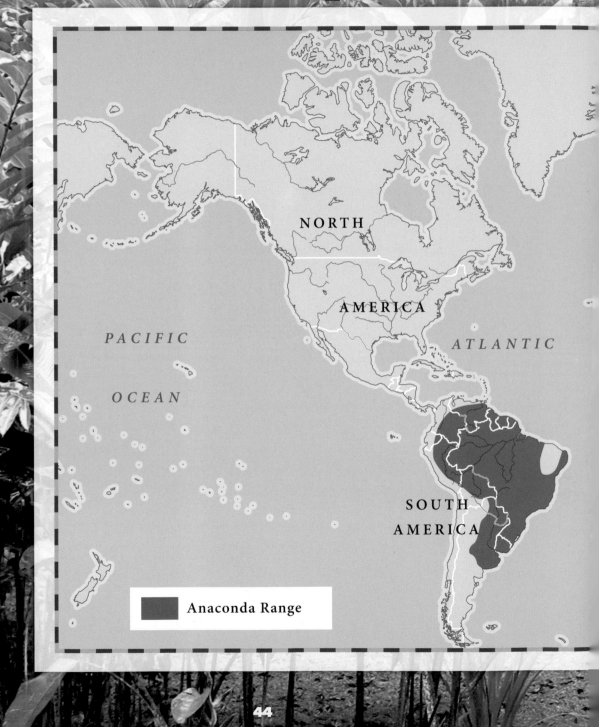

NORTH

AMERICA

PACIFIC

OCEAN

ATLANTIC

SOUTH
AMERICA

▬ Anaconda Range

ARCTIC OCEAN

EUROPE

ASIA

AFRICA

PACIFIC OCEAN

OCEAN

INDIAN OCEAN

AUSTRALIA

Find Out More

Books

Bell, Samantha. *Anaconda*. Ann Arbor, MI: Cherry Lake Publishing, 2014.

Stewart, Melissa. *Snakes!* Washington, DC: National Geographic, 2009.

Woodward, John. *Everything You Need to Know about Snakes*. New York: DK Publishing, 2013.

Visit this Scholastic Web site for more information on anacondas:
www.factsfornow.scholastic.com
Enter the keyword **Anacondas**

Index

Page numbers in *italics* indicate a photograph or map.

About the Author

Josh Gregory is the author of more than 90 books for kids. He has written about everything from animals to technology to history. A graduate of the University of Missouri–Columbia, he currently lives in Portland, Oregon.

31901065496897